BETWEEN HER TEETH

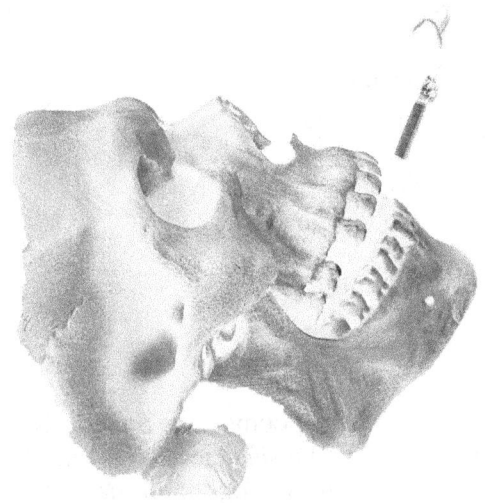

Poems by
Mela Blust

Between Her Teeth
©2022 Mela Blust
First edition. Printed in the USA.

Six Ft. Swells Press
www.sixftswellspress.com
facebook.com/SixFtSwells
Instagram: sixftswellspress

Editor: Todd Cirillo
www.toddcirillo.com

Book Design: Julie Valin
www.selftoshelfpublishing.com

Versions of some of these poems have previously appeared in *The Gasconade Review, Versification Magazine, Resurrections Mag, Horror Sleaze Trash, Neologism Journal* and *The Hellebore*.

All rights reserved. No part of this book may be reproduced in any mannor without written permission except in the case of brief quotations included in critical essays, reviews and articles.

ISBN: 978-0-9853075-9-2

Contents

wild things 1
unfuck me 2
tidal 3
i am learning 4
romance 5
everyone remembers the first time they realize
   how truly fucked up they are 6
spring has unfurled 7
once i was at a party 8
today 9
i ache 10
high 11
a fighting chance 12
dear daughter 13
fair trade 14
my cup runneth 15
dead rabbits 16
once 17
mouthful of knives 18
pretty girl 19
split personality 20
in the end 21
temptation 22
searching 23
in saying goodbye 24
we were 25
before i ever lived 26
temptation 27
lately 28
i don't like small talk 29
home 30
mela 31

perspective 32
it is no small feat 33
darkness 34
whisper 35
resilience 36
amazing 37
i've barely held my head above water 38
faith 39
last night 40
irony 41
gravity 42
plans 43
what love is 44
i am 45
seasons 46
you ask me 47
in my mind 48
and when i told you that i wanted to be broken 49
why are people drawn to the ocean? 50
this flower of guilt 51
fishing off season 52
bright flowers 53
the hunger 54
the nature of the beast 55

THE BRUTAL AND THE BEAUTY

A good writer always strives to present the reader with a reflection of the wonderful, the wild, the weird and even those moments that are all-out wrong. The poems in *Between Her Teeth* do just that. To experience the honesty of the writer poured onto the page in such a naked and sometimes beautiful, often brutal, manner makes the reader take notice.

Mela confronts the vulnerability of life's variables in these poems: the fears, the fuck-ups, one-night stands, finding the one truest love, the fragile struggle of self, freeing oneself, and figuring out how much of the world to expose to her daughter.

There is a grit to this collection that will not wash off, no matter how sweet the soap.

The fact that Mela has put these poems to paper provides the reader with a companion to keep going, whether we are in a moment of darkness or light, however it may turn out.

      - Todd Cirillo, poet, editor
      11:17p.m. 4/9/22

"But isn't it true that an author can write only about himself?"

–Milan Kundera

Between Her Teeth

WILD THINGS

i once drove by
an eight-point buck
walking right down
the middle of the road

the sodium lights
bathing his antlers
in a dusky orange glow.

as i passed,
i slowed down
to look at him and
he too, slowed
to look at me.

i think we both knew
the other
was just as wild.

UNFUCK ME

you seek my body
your hand on my face
turning it away to enter me

i am immediately responsive.
you feel my warmth in your bones
the lack of eye contact taboo –

almost more intimate than seeking my eyes
sometimes it's rough, the way i like it
tonight, soft, like you need

when it's rough, i scream
as the pain bites into me
tonight, faced with tenderness, i sob

racked with shudders until you're done
i wonder if you understand why i cry when
you're gentle
i wonder if you notice how something can
become

exactly what it isn't.

TIDAL

i want someone
to keep coming back for me
the way the tide grasps
for the shore

and sure enough, like the shore,
i will mesh with your hungry body
and then push you away
again and again.

I AM LEARNING

to leave desire alone
to observe instead
of cultivate.

my father used to tell me,
troll the line
to catch the fish

but we aren't in
the same ocean
anymore.

these days, i let sleek bodies
trail behind me
without needing
to catch every single one.

ROMANCE

on our first date, he was
a perfect gentleman,
fed me strawberries
and held my hand.

on our second date
the tension between us
balanced like the beads of
sweat on our brows.

he said he wanted me
in the worst way-
so, i got sloppy blackout drunk
tangled myself up in his sheets
and fell asleep.

i don't know
if that's what he meant
but he's never once complained.

EVERYONE REMEMBERS THE FIRST TIME THEY REALIZE HOW TRULY FUCKED UP THEY ARE

i started unbuttoning my blouse
to show the police officer
the tops of my breasts;

kept unbuttoning to indicate
that i would go all the way
to avoid this altercation.

i was young and stupid
doing 50 in a 40
with a tiny baggie of blow
tucked in my pocket.

he placed his hand
delicately onto my own
and said "stop speeding honey,
i don't need to see anything."

in my head, i knew
i'd won the game,
gotten out of a ticket
or worse.

yet, in my loins, a pathetic,
persistent tingling
in my heart,
an empty sadness

that a man
had turned down
seeing my tits.

SPRING HAS UNFURLED

and the swallowtails
have hatched

and i smile to myself
thinking about how people
romanticize having a butterfly
land on them.

as i watch
a beautiful blue-winged one

land on a pile
of shit.

ONCE I WAS AT A PARTY

having a roll in the sheets
with a man
i barely knew.

twelve minutes in
he heard the voice
of the girl he was in love with
and threw me out of bed.

i wasn't mad,
maybe a little disappointed
but i had to see the competition
for myself.

i peered through the blinds
to watch her arrive,
a raven-haired beauty
not unlike myself
but at least a foot taller

and there must have been
a metaphor there
but i was too drunk to see it,
so i slipped out the back door
and followed the train tracks
home.

TODAY

the morning
is a mountain,
heavy with the residue
of yesterday
the salt of him
still on my lips
but his body
gone away.

i had a dream
i was drowning
and the drops
are still on my limbs
every wave
a sultry flood
of him.

i'll lay back,
let the current
take me,
open wide
and just
breathe in.

I ACHE

for you
like the hunter
for his prey

knowing that some days
will bring abundance
and some,

nothing at all.
i yearn for you
like a fisherman

for his catch
patient,
but hungry.

HIGH

i want to go to where the Ferris wheel is,
steal the breeze,
take it into my lungs like the delighted squeals
of a thousand children before me.
there's nothing that makes anyone feel more
alive
than being three stories
above the ocean pounding its furious fist
against the shore.
gulls crying, wind howling,
i want to go to where there was joy,
soak it all up until i'm full.
surfboards and tanned arms holding
a thousand cigarette smoke secrets,
ice cream cone dreams,
and wave-crest wishes.
i love it up here
it hurts
less than down there.
down there they see
the glow in your eyes
and its suspect,
but up here
up here it's ok
to be
high.

A FIGHTING CHANCE

i've died
at least a thousand times
since yesterday.
and i don't ever like
to admit
the stronghold
that love has
on my soul,
but you
put me in a chokehold.
and I tapped out
without ever
throwing a punch.

DEAR DAUGHTER

my hands
have learned
how to hold you,
just so,
measuring your
small body
and your tears
to gauge
just how much truth
about the world
you can handle
at this time.

FAIR TRADE

we used to rise to the dawn
our spirits elegantly entwined.
now we climb from each night
like passengers from a wrecked ship.
there is no sweetness
left upon your lips.
there are no handprints scribbled
like scripture upon my hips.
you can seduce the bedsheets now,
i'll be gone by the time you wake.
i've never been good at negotiating,
I've never been one to settle,
So, what i propose is this –
i'll keep the memory,
and I'll let you live
with the sharp ache.

MY CUP RUNNETH

the weight gathers steadily;
drops accumulating into pools
until

all is full,
and everything spills over,
drowning what lies below.

nature waits for
nothing.

DEAD RABBITS

it was December or January, or February.
they all looked the same,
sounded the same.
the violent quiet of snow
blanketed everything
sleeping underneath.

for days we watched
the white trapping everything
in silent embrace.
each day,
wrapped our feet
for a long icy walk
out to the meadow,
carrying feed, water,
fresh straw and hay
to keep life going.

On the last day,
we walked back,
weathering the storm
as best we could,
carrying dead rabbits
like the only treasures
left to find.

ONCE

i stood naked
under the wide
unblinking sky,
and asked god
to send me a sign.

i waited, disappointed,
for a few minutes,
snuffed out my cigarette,
and went to bed.
and the sign –
or, lack thereof,
was the gift
of not wasting
a single moment
believing in anything
other
than this moment
I have to myself.

MOUTHFUL OF KNIVES

i'm still trying to shed you
from my skin.
you're a mouthful of knives
and i'm a handful of sin.
how can i get you out
if you were never in?

i beg my body to release you
your never-kiss from my lips.
such a miserable thing
to love you;
imaginary bruises
on my hips.

we get a little drunk
and go to bed again.
we bleed and bleed
and bleed
and shadow comes for us
in the end.

PRETTY GIRL

two people,
one playground ride,
everyone wants
to hop on.

watch us be
a see-saw now –
one is always up,
the other always down.

i guess you know by now
it's one or the other,
we don't both get
to come up.

well, we always knew
you'd make me more
by taking pieces away
from you.

SPLIT PERSONALITY

i am
two women
now;
the one who
drinks too much,
smokes too many
cigarettes,
stays up far too late,
and loves you…

and then the one
who knows better.

IN THE END

we were just two fools
high on dopamine
rambling back and forth
about love
and poetry
and death
and anything else
we could
to take up time
and space.

TEMPTATION

sometimes
i can see the hole
i'll fall into
below
and simultaneously
see the rope
that will save me
dangling above
and how the hole
is much more tempting
than the rope.

SEARCHING

when i was four years old
my mother took me blackberry picking,
and as i leaned over the edge
of the lake,
an alligator's perfect ivory teeth
rushed up from
the ghost-dark depths
for a meal.

i stumbled backwards in fear,
narrowly escaping
a premature death.
i have never forgotten
that image;
but i remember thinking
how beautiful he was.

years later i glide
through the Everglades
in a canoe,
throwing deli ham into the water
for the gators,
still searching
for beauty
just as dangerous.

IN SAYING GOODBYE

you've taught me
perhaps
the greatest lesson
of all

that friendship
is not having a friend
but
being a friend.

as i realize that i am more hurt
by the thought of your suffering
than my own
in losing you.

WE WERE

everything
and nothing
and all at once

a thousand supercharged
dopamine receptors
of outstretched, welcoming arms.

your eyes held jewels
both brilliant
and tragic.

i looked into them
and saw
what could be,
what I wanted to be
and you

looked into mine
and ran
away.

BEFORE I EVER LIVED

i remember leaning
my flushed pink face
against the glass

and whispering
take me
please take me

before i learned
that no one was coming
and no one
will save me.

TEMPTATION

the sugar of life
i already have
all i need

and still
want more

i don't think

i could have it
any better
but my brain

sure likes
to suggest
that i could.

LATELY

i never understood
why people called sex
making love.

in my twenties
meeting a man i hardly knew
for fifteen minutes
of breathless passion
it hardly seemed like making
anything resembling love
to me.

lately, love seems to be
in every doorway
holding hands,
locking eyes,
tension in the air.

lately i imagine
that most of my life
is making
love.

I DON'T LIKE SMALL TALK

i don't want to talk
about the news
or traffic
or your shit job,

i want to dig
into the meat of you
and disappear
into your depth,

i want the waters
muddied
and your fingers
laced in mine,

i want to laugh
until our sides hurt
leaving us
hungry for more.

HOME

it's always fascinating
to learn
who lives inside
of houses.
how they can have
bright gardens
and flowers hanging
on the door.

a bright façade
for a darker truth
that despite the flowers
the people inside
still
hurt each other
again and again.

MELA

means darkness in Greek.
it means that i
am no longer afraid.

when my friends ride with me
in my car
they hold on tight
and say god damn mama
and i tap the brake
for their sake.

alone, i lean hard
into the curves
downshift, and hit the gas
i am not afraid of going down
over the embankment
and flying into my demise.

instead i fantasize about
how i'd scream
like a motherfucker
and then whisper softly
to death
honey,
i'm coming home.

PERSPECTIVE

there is a spider
struggling,
lost among the infinite
black tendrils
of my hair
and i know that
it is important to remember
that he doesn't want to be there
anymore
than i want him there.

IT IS NO SMALL FEAT

to feel your finger
trace the back of my thigh
up
to the point
of delirium,
and just keep walking
through the grocery store.
you ask me what aisle
the bottled water is on,
and i tell you there is an ocean
between my thighs.

DARKNESS

his hands run through
my raven hair
pointing out
a tiny streak
of brown,

he says
"you can only see it
in the sunlight."

later, he finds me naked
in the bathroom
dying my hair again.

i tell him
i want my hair as black
as my soul.

he kisses my shoulder
and says,
"i didn't know they made dye
that black."

WHISPER

"you're like an angel,"
he whispered,
with his hand
on my thigh,

his cerulean eyes
gazing
into mine.

i smiled coyly
as he came in
for a kiss

thinking to myself
that lucifer
was an angel too.

RESILIENCE

i whispered a plea to my heart
to keep going
and somehow
it did.

at some point
you will gaze out of a window
at some horizon beyond

and when you turn back
you'll turn around to some life
other than the one you remember
and pleaded for.

AMAZING

my husband watches me
twist my long black hair
into a bun and secure it
without any instrument,
only wrapping it up
in itself.

"it's so amazing how
you do that," he says.

later, standing behind me,
he wraps his fist up
so tight in my hair
that playfully trying
to escape his grasp
is impossible

leaving me
with absolutely no desire
to escape.

i think to myself,
"it's so amazing
how you do that.

I'VE BARELY HELD MY HEAD ABOVE WATER

for so long
no one but you
could understand

why i giggled
when we wrestled playfully
in the hot tub

and you held my head
under water
for just a few seconds

somehow you, too, knew
that i was intimate
with drowning.

FAITH

i lay my head down
on your chest
listening to the powerful thudding
of your heart

and although you passed
your last physical
with flying colors

to suddenly think
that the fist-sized organ
i'm hearing
is responsible for the livelihood
of every inch
of the person i love most

is too fragile
to believe.

LAST NIGHT

as my limbs
lay tangled in yours
we heard rumbling.

we paused,
exchanged glances
and then
you went back
under the sheets.

the next day
i heard many say
that there was a fiery
comet tearing through
the night sky.

a friend joked
that i missed the
explosion.

oh, no,
i think to myself,
i definitely saw the sky
light up.

IRONY

it doesn't escape me
that i was so angry at you
for lying to me,

yet all the while
i asked you to lie to me
every single night

when i curled up in your arms
and begged you to tell me
that everything would be ok.

GRAVITY

you
have proven to be
the darkest hole
i've ever fallen into.
the descent
is maddening,
and laced
with all the most
delicious sins.
and i
am not even trying
to escape.

PLANS

i'm going out tonight,
i don't need a dress.
my face will do the talking,
my body, the rest.
loneliness is a paper doll
i keep undressing
with my eyes.
but my mouth
gets me into trouble.
and lord knows,
so do my thighs.

WHAT LOVE IS

funny how
the reaching of a hand
can be the bridge
across an ocean
of misunderstanding.

you with your headache
that i thought was anger,
my lips sealed tightly
to appease you.
my heart in anguish
knowing that you still
carry the weight
of what i've done.

and you smile wearily,
thumbing my palm,
and tell me
how bad it hurts.
and i nod,
and whisper
i'm sorry baby.

I AM

lonely candlelight
in a window
that you'll never see

i'll let you
light the flame —
you'll gladly
start the fire

and you'll get
to smell the smoke
but someone else

will always
have to extinguish
the flames.

SEASONS

a long cold winter
had me forget
the work of the land,

covered in sweat and dirt
and unsure
of the line

where the earth ends
and my body
begins.

winter's fingers had me forget
that the line
doesn't exist.

YOU ASK ME

does the sadness still linger
under the surface
when you are smiling?
it does.
when i am smiling
when i am laughing
when i am anything
at all.
i can only chase it away
with dopamine.
So, lift my spirits
lift my skirt,
i will play with you,
pray with you,
fuck you
and it'll be there
like a counselor
like a priest
like a bad threesome.
The most honest answer
i can give is to
learn to love my sadness
as much as i love you
and as much as i believe,
it
loves me.

IN MY MIND

i already know
every inch of you,
the smell of your skin
the taste of your mouth.

you've already been
inside me –
explored the darkest corners
of my depths.

i've already had you
many times,
and still there remains all the ways
in which i can't actually have you.

i've said everything
we both want to hear.

so, if you're waiting
for the words –
don't hold your breath
and i won't hold mine,
i've already told you
in my mind.

AND WHEN I TOLD YOU THAT I WANTED TO BE BROKEN

you reveled in my submission, drank it

with the thirst of a man whose tongue
had never touched nectar

but you used your hands:

you pulled my crow's-wing hair,
you bruised my feather quill neck.

what i meant was this—break me open,
spill this ugliness sleeping inside me

i wanted the monster out of me so badly
that i was willing to risk it
discovering you.

WHY ARE PEOPLE DRAWN TO THE OCEAN?

my mother asks,
crying into the Gulf of Mexico,
sending her teardrops home—
a burial at sea.

earlier, we sat bone-still,
listening to a room of lonely people
whisper my father into a graveless death—
a pile of ash

and although
we rarely speak of how the choice
was made,

i know now
that we don't bury the body for the body,
but for the digging.

THIS FLOWER OF GUILT

is a thorn-ripped hole,
a blood-pool where i throw things
never to be seen again
i will revisit the hole
like a twisted wishing well
every single day
for years
and after a time,
it shapeshifts
into something like
guilt

because i'm still here
and you are not.

FISHING OFF SEASON

there were ripples
just under the surface
and i was attracted
to the light,

so you let me in
just enough
to get me hooked
and then

you tore me off
and threw me back.

BRIGHT FLOWERS

i know there is still
some buried beauty
waiting to spring up
from my darkest heart,

the way
bright flowers
are found
in dark cemeteries.

THE HUNGER

I used to be afraid
of black widows—
the elusive leggy creatures
remind me of myself.

she casts a wide net,
hoping to catch something,
anything
to use, to entrap,
to devour alive
until she is alone again.

but if shit gets too real
and something more predatory
gives chase
she turns
and runs away
hiding in dark places
until, once again,
the hunger
becomes too great.

THE NATURE OF THE BEAST

my dog looks at me incredulously
as i scream at her
to release the hen
in her mouth.

i understand now
this is how we move
differently
in the world.

to me,
she is the beast.
to her,
she holds the beast
between her teeth.

MELA BLUST is an award nominated poet, sculptor, jeweler, and artist. She is partially feral, and can probably drink you under the table. More of Mela's work can be found floating around the internet.

After Hours Poetry

Support the small press!

Six Ft. Swells has been publishing poetry books and collections since 2005, with the goal of making poetry accessible, interactive and fun.

sixftswellspress.com

facebook.com/SixFtSwells

instagram.com/sixftswellspress

Other Six Ft. Swells Press Titles:

www.ingramcontent.com/pod-product-compliance
Lightning Source LLC
Chambersburg PA
CBHW071750040426
42446CB00012B/2512